This book is a special collection of selected poems and lyrics by Valerie Lumley and James Tippey, AKA Garland Andrews.

The verses represent the events and relationships of their lives, are presented in chronological order, and are combined in two parts.

They are soulful and intimate, and even whimsical. They describe life and love in its many forms and expressions, tell stories that are profound and real, and testify to forms of love that are transcendent and eternal.

Zephyrs In The Spring

A special collection of selected poems & lyrics -

*By Valerie Lumley and
James Tippey,
AKA Garland Andrews*

2020 - Monterey, California

ALL RIGHTS RESERVED © 2020 BY VALERIE LUMLEY

The poetry of Garland Andrews was bequeathed to Valerie upon his death.

No part of this book may be reproduced or transmitted in any form or by any means, electronic or mechanical, including photocopying, recording, or by any information storage and retrieval system, without permission in writing from the publisher.

FOR MORE INFORMATION
PLEASE VISIT: SETONPUBLISHING.COM

ISBN-13: 978-1-7349057-2-4

Visit the author's website: valerielumley.com to see her other books.

- The INappropriate Therapist
- The Grand Master And His Protégé
- Curing Chronic Fibromyalgia

INTERIOR AND COVER DESIGN BY VALERIE LUMLEY

PRINTED IN THE UNITED STATES OF AMERICA

Dedication

This book is dedicated to all you hidden inner-poets out there, waiting to come out, come out, wherever you are!

Valerie Lumley

Valerie is a pioneer business entrepreneur, a trained classical soprano, a published author, and a poet in her own mind.

She lives happily in Monterey, California with her husband of 30 years, along with her family; two African parrots, Mozart and Poquito, her Australian cockatiel, Jake, and two rescue doggies, Nina and Ricky. She loves spending time with her husband, walking on the local beaches with their dogs, singing, writing, painting, and gardening.

* * *

James Tippey, AKA Garland Andrews

Garland was Valerie's beloved surrogate father, mentor, voice teacher, cultural soulmate, and musical and artistic inspiration.

This book is to remember that he was not only a great American baritone, a brilliant teacher, composer, musician, and conductor of his own symphony, but also an award-winning poet. It was a karmic miracle that Garland and Valerie found each other again after life separated them for 40-years.

He will always be loved and missed!
(November 26, 1931 – December 13, 2016)

CONTENTS
Part one
Valerie Lumley

The Willow Tree	2
The Sky	3
Singing Lady	4
Fruit Trees & Feathers	5
Goodbye Gregory	6
Fisherman	7
Angels	8
To Love	10
Something I've Got To Do	11
The Sea	12
A Point In Time	14
A Special Kind Of Love	15
A Stranger To Your Heart	17
Choices	19
Gentle Hearts	20
Journey To The Garden	22
I Say Goodbye	25
To Jan	27
Freedom Light	28
Phoenix Rising	30
On Golden Threads	31
The Spirit Gardener	32
The Owl & The Nightingale	34
A Man I've Loved	35
Without You	37
A Lifetime Of Richness	38
The Lioness	41
The Gift Of Avelyn	42

Part Two
James Tippey,
AKA Garland Andrews

Love's Analysis	45
Winterrhyme	46
Epistle	47
Ode To The Setting Sun	48
The Children's Home	49
Otis	51
Father Of Her Child	53
The Long Night Wake*	55
The Countess Of Manhattan	56
Impersonal Acquaintance	59
Mother-Child	61
The Very Touch Of You	65
San Francisco Rose	67
The Lucid Pool	70
The Image Of Me	71
Eros' Wine	70
The Road Less Traveled	73
Peccavi*	74
Silent Pleas	75
To Valeria	76
Two Girls Went To Church	77
A Walk In The Sun	79
Dogs And Cats	81
Parrots - Or A Tribute To Mozart	83
Thoughts Worth Repeating	84
Dearest Love	85
Return And Farewell	86

The End Of The Line	87
Gifts Of The Magi	88
Many Wondrous Sounds	89
A Zephyr In The Spring	90
My Darling Valerie	92
Reasons I Love You	93
Love Of Mine	94

Award-winning poems*

PART ONE

Poems & lyrics
by Valerie Lumley

The Willow Tree

I love you glimmering in the sun;
its shadows casting through your hair.
As you return the sun's caress,
you stand more proudly than other's dare.

I love you when the wind is soft
and you dance there flowing free.
You grow and bend and touch the sky;
you seem to live just for me.

I love you when the nights are dark and
the moon's light peeks through your boughs.
Your limbs are outstretched, reaching tall;
no other tree can compare to thou.

I love you when I'm sad and lone;
you shelter me under your wing.
I feel your calm and loving tones.
I hear the songs you sing.

1969
At age 17

The Sky

Time and time we talk of love
and try to love all we can.
But how often do we walk the beach
and talk about the sand?

We are companions in a dream,
we hold our dream so high.
But like all dreams they are hard to know
so we cry about the sky.

Now and then we talk of love
and try to know each other.
But different is our dream of love
from a love we should share together.

And now you're going far away;
our dream will be offended.
I'll walk the beaches every day
and I'll know that our love has ended.

1969

Singing Lady

*Singing lady, laughing lady,
what do you think today?
Living longer, growing stronger;
so what's the use of you today?*

*Shall we walk and talk in the wind?
Your secrets will blow to the hills.
Show me now your soul within.
Can you empty your heart as it fills?*

*Tell me softly, tell me truly;
what do you see in your mind?
Merry men, or gentlemen,
or a noble – one of a kind?*

*Why is a sparkle afloat in your eye?
Has a memory strummed its chord?
I'll promise the earth to live or die
to feel all emotion you can afford.*

*Singing lady, somber lady;
do you miss something gone from the past?
Presently seen, memories dream
lives inside you, at last.*

*Must an ocean swell between us
all at once in the face of this life?
Today is better, there's less to fear.
Your thoughts are at ease in the night.*

1975

Fruit Trees & Feathers

Only lonely people come here.
They bring flowers and tears,
and confessions from the years
they've left behind.

My heart shares the sorrow
of the lonely widow.
How she's pale in her face.
No one else can take his place.

I know in your sorrow,
you feel closer to him; and you do.
To see him there in your memory's eye,
makes you sad and you know that it's true.

If you imagine them where
it is cold with no air,
you'll turn around and
he'll not be in view.

But if you see them in flowers,
in fruit trees and feathers,
he'll be there, always there,
ever comforting you.

So if I see you in a starlit sky,
or in a field of mustard, I'll not ask why.
You fill the deep oceans
and caress the high mountains.
You are life, you are life, you and I.

1975

Goodbye, Gregory

Goodbye, Gregory.
I see you're sailing out to sea.
You said all things are meant to be.
You said it so convincingly.

Sail away, Gregory.
You've sharpened all my memory.
You showed me what life has for me.
So set your sail for all to see.

I know, Gregory,
the things you gave so splendidly.
You thought of me so lovingly.
I'll not forget what you said to me.

"You're so good inside,
and you'll always be.
And there'll come a day
when it's that you'll see."
And then I knew that he knew me.

I know, Gregory;
there'll come a day that's meant for me.
A day predicted seldomly;
I'll find you on the great salt sea.

And setting sail for all to see,
we'll sail away, sail away, sail away,
Gregory.

1976
For Gregory
(1950 - 1970)

Fisherman

Fisherman, you love the sea.
Fisherman, you love me.

You said your love's like a
swell or a wave, a calm or a storm,
but you knew you were
born for the sea.

You know who you are;
a sparkle from a star.

But I have imagined
the sea as a phantom,
when you imagine
the sea as your father.
So, why do you bother
to promise me love?

I will not take you from
something that is you.
And could you be torn
between the sea and me?

Maybe you just want me
to make up your mind, or,
maybe you're just using me.

But I'll always know
that you came from the sea.

1976

Angels

Have you ever seen an angel?
Has one ever spoken to you?
It seems unlikely, but I have;
in a dream it all came true.

I laid on my bed by the light of the moon
and I wanted to feel some peace.
I floated away from reality,
and I dreamed of exhaustion and heat.

I longed to see a cool waterfall
and some ferns to please my eye.
I decided that I was suffering,
so I began to cry.

An angel came from behind me
and another from above.
Their faces fair with silken hair;
they radiated love.

Their wings as they floated through the
air; such beauty I'd never seen.
So large, so full, white feathers fair;
I was sorry t'was merely a dream.

With the grace of swans in a bold ballet,
they surrounded me, and I heard one say:

"Lay on my bed of golden down,
I'll fan you with my wings."

The other brushed my face with snow
and told me many things.

"There are worlds beyond and wonders
high"... that God has kept from me.
"Would you like to fly with us a while?
The moon and beyond you will see."

I feared I would not return somehow
and I knew that I best not go.
Such pleasure and rest they gave me there
and I graciously told them so.

I don't believe in Angels or
in God as I've heard them to be.
But if ever were angels known to man,
they'd have been as they were to me.

1976

To Love

All of my life I've needed love.
All of my life I tried to give it.
But love, you confuse me
when I need you to amuse me
and to comfort my soul.

So, my reason is a cage
for my wildest emotions
that want to run free
to hunt down my devotions.

I know what can be lost
if you tempt me with desires.
You want to tie me to your back
with your invisible wires.

You want to carry me away
and leave me little or no control.
But I'm wise to you now,
though you've captured my soul.

I need to see you as you are
and not be blinded by your star.
I need to look you in the eye
so I know you when I die.

Oh love, be gentle to me now
and understand me when I say;
I want you with me
as I live from day to day.

1977

Something I've Got To Do

There's something that I've got to do.
I could put it off, but what's the use?
I know I'll not be satisfied till I begin.

You have faith in me, this I know.
And you'll stand by me, you told me so.
You said, "I'll be so proud of you
when you begin."

There's just one thing that I want to say;
you don't know my fears,
you don't live my day.
Though I see you looking at me with pride;
try looking at it from my side.

Sometimes I feel like giving it up;
knowing I'll always feel hallow inside;
losing my pride; I should have tried.

Stay with me baby and tell I'll make it.
Don't say that I'm worthy,
just tell me you care.
I know I can do it, well,
I know that I'll try to.
Fulfillment's is living,
and it's living I dare.

There's something that I've got to do;
Oh baby, let me share it with you.

1978

The Sea

The sea is a subject
that writers compose.
The singer will sing it
from verses he knows.
A poet can capture the
moods of the sea,
like a painting so vivid to me.

The ocean has depth
and a varying tide.
It carries the vessels for fish to abide.
It takes life and gives it;
its fate it will call
in a melody beaconing all.

The sky and the heavens
reflect on the sea
a colorful blue or a gray harmony.
Its endless horizons will
swallow you whole.
It gives time for soothing the soul.

The magical sounds that
come in with the tide
are telling their story
and seeming alive.
They generate feelings
from deep in the heart.
And my friend,
that's a good place to start.

I go to the sea when I feel a bit blue,
or wanting to think about
the things that I do.
It simplifies living to breathing in air.
Such peace it will give you to share.

1979

A Point In Time

*At any time within in my life,
from all I am through grief and strife;*

*On whatever path in any season,
in any light illuminating any reason;*

*In whatever setting on any day,
from whatever philosophy
is showing the way;*

*Amidst any circumstance
or crisis born, or however
unpredictable the storm;*

*In desire's passion, or love's illusion,
in joy's splendor, or sorrow's confusion;*

*Any point in time you crossed my path;
I would have stopped
and given you my love.*

1981

A Special Kind Of Love

*I've spent a lifetime searching for
a special kind of love.
With one who is unusual;
the kind I understand.*

*I've known some other men before
and tried to love a few.
But none had near the qualities
I've only seen in you.*

*I look into your eyes
and I feel I've found my home.
I want to spend my life with you
and long to see your smile.*

*I care about your happiness
and what is best for you.
I care about your problems
and I want to be your friend.*

*I believe in you.
So simple, but true.
I love you more than ever I
loved a man before.*

*I see how life is changing you;
how realistic you've become.
I want to be a part of it
and share what I can with you.*

*I know you will always learn
life's lessons as you grow.*

*I also know you'll always be
the finest kind of man.*

*I've never wanted any man
the way that I want you.
I know I never have admired
a man this much before.*

*I wish life could be easier,
but that's my own point of view.
If only fate would be so kind
as to twist our way.*

*I believe in you.
So simple, but true.
I love you more than ever I
loved a man before.*

1984

A Stranger To Your Heart

I am a stranger to your heart.
You cannot see me yet.
I've tried to convey how
safe you are with me.

You look at me
and your eyes see the shadows
of your heart's secret corners.
Places that remember joy.
Places that house virulent pain.

You see only my refraction
through these shadowy viscosities.
You wait for the shadows to pass;
shadows my heart, too, has within.

Through this inner prism
I see your form and I care.
I observe with gentle comprehension.
You perceive your own image
reflected back from me.

I am none of the mirrors
you've looked into before.
I polish my surface with truth
to evade distortion.

With this same truth,
I assess the image of myself
reflected back by you.

I am open, and
as life washes through me
my inner world diversifies.

When I am with you
I share what I have
and the content is mine.
I do not want to rob your inner store.

So, as a stranger to your heart –
a shadowy reflection
of your heart's secret corners –
you try to see me.

And as the moments change,
the tenderness we share
creates acuity.

The shadows return,
only to dispel with time,
and the clouded viscosities
surrender again to clarity.

1988

Choices

As time goes by
and we live out our lives,
we do not share them.
I do not see you except
for in one eternal moment.

Although my mind is occupied
and my light shines brightly,
there remains an exiled self
that survives deep within me,
where joy is inspired and felt,
yet is cloaked with the sadness
of life's cruel dualities.

As our love remain,
unchanged by choices
or fate's twisted fortune,
acceptance can only appease
without expectation of change.

As we live out our lives,
I will always feel you in my heart
and see you in my mind,
knowing only what could have been,
and was not chosen.

1988

Gentle Hearts

When I see you in my dreams
your eyes look deeply into mine.
I can hear you speaking to me softly.
Although I am alone, you are with me.

You have entered my heart,
and you hold me tenderly there.
Your kind nature soothes my tired soul,
and my best self
that had become a stranger to me
has come to life again.

I want to hope
and believe in dreams again.
Life should not be without these.
You are so easy to love
and so deserving of it.

You softly move mountains of despair
and cause them to vanish in silence.
You inspire love. You grace my life.
You gently are what
strong men try to be.

Don't ever change.
You will go with me
should life guide us apart.

I will never leave you behind
like others who have entered my heart
and vanished in time.

With you, time does not exist.
You are the joy, the hope,
and the love that life has to offer.

In your gentle ways
you are all these things.
Thank you for being this to me.
I do love you so.

1990
For Ron

Journey To The Garden

I grew up in a vast wasteland of despair
that bordered on a great abyss.
I felt alone and afraid.

I had only one hand to hold on to.
It was the hand of my brother.
One day he was killed
and I began to wander.

Lost and empty, within a
dark and turbulent storm,
I tumbled down into the abyss.

After many years in darkness,
a light began to dimly flicker.

I looked ahead and saw my own path,
and I knew that the light
was coming from within me.

I looked back and saw the face of evil,
and decided to go my own way.

With all I had
I slowly climbed the jagged edge
and never looked back again.

I did not lose heart,
but began to lose hope.
And as I reached the top
I felt the warmth of my brother's love.

And when I held out my hand
it was met by another.

This hand began leading me
on what would become
a long journey through an arid
and treacherous wasteland
toward a wondrous, beautiful garden.

Such a place I had never seen.
Along the way my light began
to sparkle and glow,
and as I grew nearer,
I saw farther and clearer
than ever before.

My heart began to fill with hope,
and my soul began to sing.
I knew that this garden was
where I truly belonged,
and I felt it was my brother
who'd lead me there.

And now when I enter this garden,
I want to sing with joy and gratitude
and touch the hearts of all
who hear my song.

I want to climb to the treetops
and watch the eagles soar.
I want to hear the earth-music in the wind
and be a part of the miracle
of creating heaven on earth.

*It is a lot to desire, but each day I hope
this dream will become the truth,
and what was true before
will become the dream.*

*I strive to become strong enough
to be the person I am meant to be,
fulfilling a long-awaited destiny.*

1999

I Say Goodbye

I say goodbye to an innocent buried.
I say goodbye to a childhood missed.
I say goodbye to the unseen blossom
and the twisted vine by
the dew not kissed.

I say goodbye
to a poisoned youth.
I say goodbye as it finally ends.
I turn my back and am not defeated.
I boldly go where the road now bends.

I say goodbye
to the beguiled young beauty.
I say goodbye as she lived unknown.
I say goodbye to old dreams escaping
and to the pearl whose host
was blindly sewn.

I say goodbye
to the misplaced promise.
I say goodbye to the years that died;
to the terror and mercy
and pain repeated;
to the untrained pilot
who charmed and lied.

I say goodbye
to the spirit shredder;
to the grizzly's claws
as its grasp uncurls.

*I see its retreat
and its dissipation,
and the lifeless pose
of its face unfurled.*

*I say goodbye
to the unknown God,
to the un-kept faith,
and the un-felt trust;
to the blind man's staff,
and the warlord's treasure.*

*I leap from the mountain,
as I know I must.*

1999

To Jan – from Rex

*I'm walking on a new byway;
along the waters of all my days.*

*I see the landscape I leave behind;
the peaks and valleys
of what was mine.*

*I've no regrets for what I am;
the simple things for which I stand.*

*I feel my triumphs that may be few
have largely come from loving you.*

*And when I failed it may be said,
I gained ten times from what I shed.*

*So with this prayer I give my thanks
for how I moved among the ranks.*

*Because of what you were to me
the worth of life is all I see.*

2004 – Channeled from Rex to Jan

Two weeks after he died.

Freedom Light

Within the sorrow of what almost was,
the visions in my soul are like zephyrs
that float through my being like ghosts;
ghosts from a time that was ripe
with splendid joy; tragic,
epic, and forever.

A time that endowed life with mystery.
A time that discovered me,
and all I could ever be was revealed
in one transient eternity.

And it was brought forth, shared,
and given with a force molten
with stern intent, instilling
the essence and strength of being.

An inner strength that, to me,
became unknown, unseen, and unfelt
while living a thrown upon life;
only to be revealed in one timely instant,
to emerge like an awakened dragon
from its restorative cave;
leaving the darkness,
spreading open its sleepy wings without,
exposing its giant, hidden heart within.

A heart that fought so bravely,
so steadfastly and heavy, while carried
among and through an un-chosen course,

*around the bends of unfriendly miles
that wound sharply into hazes
and disappeared.*

*A heart yet carried forth
to dare the journey;
to hold itself against a truer,
more intended fate.*

*A fate to find its freedom light;
to illuminate each and every struggle,
and see that the strength, the courage,
and the love intended
were only moments away
and always present within;*

*To be sought out through
this determined agony,
and claimed forever as rightful;*

*To be melded together
with every gift so freely given,
as this giant and brave heart
passes through each new and brighter day.*

2007

Phoenix Rising

*Out of the pyre of life's injustice,
from events unearned and unforeseen,
emerges a caged and broken spirit,
now injected with
the power of immortal love.*

*This spirit ascends like a shining phoenix,
up and out of its primal darkness
with a blast of comet-like force and so
furious a will that fuels its blazing wings,
as streaks of light glow wide beneath.*

*The phoenix rises and breaks free,
illuminating all that has gone before
in a single flash of comprehension,
never to sink or descend again.*

*The ignited intention of its recovered
power surges within the heart of its
reclaimed spirit, and courses through
the miles of its electrified veins,
as the magnificent phoenix
rises again as once before, when
as its truest, most incandescent self,
is unfettered by events or time.*

*Brilliant with love and consciousness,
on fire with its natural blinding
luminosity, you, the phoenix, return.*

2007

On Golden Threads

*On inhaled breath his soul is spun
on golden threads that do not fail.
Within each utterance of God's intent
he fills the hearts of all who hale.*

*With every tone his soul is rung
like bells on mountaintops do ring.
His gentle soaring voice resounds
infusing love with all he sings.*

*It matters not what line is taught,
or how the master's wrote the phrase.
This man who shows not the egos face
sings honoring only beauties praise.*

*Earth's trembling shores and dusty plains
know fully of God's will and art.
But human sight is blind to all
this man gives freely from his heart.*

*It takes a soul that senses heaven
and hears earth's silent sadness woes
through nature's choirs and living
rhythms, to inherit the magic he bestows.*

*This gentle man whose soul does spin
in velvet tones of glorious size,
so fills the inner world of she
whose joy doth give his deserved prize.*

*2011
For Garland*

The Spirit Gardener

*Before you, I was like an unseen blossom,
hidden deep beneath the overgrowth
of an unattended garden,
sustained only by what moisture
could be gathered by each dawning day.*

*You are the spirit gardener
who happened upon me by chance,
and lifted me out of the shadow
of an unknown slumber; an adaptive
hibernation of unrealized possibilities.*

*You gently placed me in fertile soil,
and showered me with pure water.
You gave me room, and sun, and shade.
You saw me for what I truly was
and encouraged me to claim myself.*

*From hardy, yet baron branches
sprang forth unsuspecting stalks
that at their ends, formed and swelled
unfamiliar buds of vibrant colors
and shapes.*

*Buds that rose up and bloomed
with the fragrance of life's buried longings
yet to be fulfilled.*

*You saw this as beautiful,
and mirrored to me the truth of it.*

You said you are a man who can take in
the fragrances you have cultivated,
as if life has given you an unexpected gift;
one that is as pure as the water you have
so lavishly showered upon my thirsty
spirit.

Yet, if all you want is to adore the blossom;
to feast your eyes upon what has grown
before you, inhale its fragrance, and feel
the emotions springing forth from this gift
you have given yourself, then I will love
you always, and remain your Nightingale.

2011
For Garland

The Owl and the Nightingale

God bless these hours that are between us now, that they may pass by with joy and safety, and deliver you to my door with confidence and love.

You are the life I should have had. You are the man of my past dreams, once dreamt in innocence before the nightmare-times came that made me feel worthless and ashamed.

I should have flown into your arms then, but I was only the young Nightingale, and you were the greatest of Owls. How could I have satisfied your hungers then?

But now, this Nightingale who has been unsung for so many years, sings again because of you, and with gratitude this time for all of life's blessings.

And so the greatest of Owls is content to listen while the tiny Nightingale sings at last under his expansive wings, and their souls are finally as one in spirit. Hold my spirit beneath your great wings, always. Amen.

July 30, 2011
For Garland

A Man I've Loved

I know you as a man I've loved. I see you like no other, and always have. Like me, you are highly sensitive and naturally intuitive with the strength of 1000 lions.

You are a primal man, unafraid of your nature. You have guided yourself through life being true to thyself in every way, in spite of those who tried to sway, inhibit, stifle, or destroy you.

You have always chosen to lift yourself above what others would consider insurmountable odds. You have never allowed fear to be your master.

Instead, you looked fear in its crude and ugly face, and seeing it for the tawdry thing it is, you rose above it and left it behind you in your conquering wake.

Your courage has been your strength, your convictions have been your armor, and your un-suppressible talent has been your sword.

You have done what most others fail to do in one lifetime. You have fought for and found your truest self, and have thus fulfilled your many callings and potential.

Women have been your nourishment and your fervor. Your children have been your solace and your reward.

You have given the world all you could give, and still, there remains an untapped magnitude more within you.

You stand above other men with quiet dignity and an honest humility that is more than necessary.

You accept my love, and return it in the same manner in which you have lived.

You have enhanced the best of me, and have freed my spirit by freeing my voice.

I will sing to you always, and I will love you for the remainder of my life.

2011
For Garland

Without You

My Darling Garland,

Without you – I would have died an unfulfilled woman.
Without you – I would never have found my truest self.
Without you – My heart would never have healed.
Without you – I would not have discovered the endless bounds of the human heart.
Without you – My life would seem a series of failures.

Thank you for all these gifts of genuine love!

I love you, always and forever,
Valerie

November 26, 2016
For Garland

On your 85th birthday –
17 days before you passed away
in my arms.

A Lifetime of Richness

You bore the pains of all mankind;
cruelty, betrayal, and loss.
While defeating the hardships of your life,
you carried your heavy cross.

And through it all your will so strong
survived all manner of trials.
Although your struggles were ever long,
you traversed each crooked mile.

No rival, foe, or enemy
who deigned to bring you down,
could stand against your majesty,
or steel your righteous crown.

For in your heart beat lion's blood
through veins of golden light.
Your glow would blind the evil ones
who dared to cause you strife.

Your spirit, blessed with rich desires,
was wise beyond your years.
Your life was fueled by what inspires
most men to cede in tears.

And through it all you sheathed your
sword, and faced your lot with grace.
Your goodness prevailed to touch the Lord,
and shone on your mother's face.

*In countless triumphs you chose being
humble, out-casting most sought-after
fame; surpassing your peers with nary a
stumble, "Stalwart" became your name.*

*Academic success was natural to you.
Being father was a gift of your love.
Your steadfastness remained anew,
no matter what life reminded you of.*

*And now, looking back, you can't help
wonder, "Just how did I do it all?"
Without even knowing that under your
shyness was stronger your natural call.*

*In every way you evolved your spirit
to the highest of human attainment.
Efforts, as failures, came nowhere near it;
as each fell into perfect alignment.*

*Looking forward you may be asking
yourself, "Just what is left for me now?"
And while you look for a worthy task,
you are far from taking a bow.*

*There is love in your life,
and more poems to write.
New adventures will dawn
as you dreams in the night.*

*Masses could proffer from
your lifetime of richness.
Such wisdom you've offered
with true and loving wishes.*

*And now your time has come and gone to leave us in this place.
And every heartbeat, breath, and tear, will hold you in love's embrace.*

February 8, 2014 – For Garland

*Garland crossed over peacefully on December 13, 2016 at 10:50 pm.
The last verse was written on December 26, 2016.*

The Lioness

Hale to the lioness!
Who ventured into the jungle
and hunted down d'evil;
chased it out into the open
and roared the truth at it.

And as she stood her ground
and weathered the fury
of evil's hate-storms,
she drew courage and strength
from her hard-fought convictions.

Afterward, she shook it all off
like stale desert dust,
and peaceably went along her way.

March 1, 2020

The Gift Of Avelyn

Your mother gave you the gift of life,
and you are life's gift to her.

Your spirit is brilliant
and sparkles with clarity.
Your life as you live it
will be filled with charity.

And as you mature
the world will surround you
with the love you were raised with;
this love will abound you.

Your talent and passion
will surprise you, no doubt.
The adventures of life
will teach all it's about.

And in every transaction
or decision you make,
will point your direction
and the path you must take.

So follow your spirit
and your heart's great desire
with full faith in yourself,
no matter what will transpire.

You see, life is for learning,
and gaining its wisdom;
to leave something behind
from your own inner prism.

Your journey is yours;
and unique as you are!
So let nothing prevent you
from following your star.

Let nothing persuade you
against what you know.
The world will be graced
by your soul as you grow.

For Avelyn comes into
a world that will need her;
and all she will give it
will transform it for better.

So, thank you, dear Avelyn,
for choosing this home!
With your parent's as guides
the right way will be shown.

Valerie Lumley
2021

PART TWO

*Poems by James Tippey,
AKA Garland Andrews*

Love's Analysis

"Love is not justice.
It is not duty; nor is it pleasure,
and yet it contains a measure
of all these things.

There are a thousand ways to feel it,
to reveal it; but for those whose souls
the mundane transcend,
and seek the absolute, it is one,
with neither beginning nor end."

Once I set this down,
I then sat back and read it--
A true je t'aime de Paris . . .
but it wasn't I who said it.

It was Liszt to Countess Marie.

*Paraphrased from a translation of the
French by Eleanor Perenyi*

James Tippey
1955
At age 24

Winterrhyme

almost a month now,
yet how long the month
since i last beheld you,
and your soul was a part of mine,
as mine was with yours.
no tender mouth now,
that on a child or spinster
would arouse the furies of hell
and cause the weak to become strong
and the strong to become tame—
by what name can it remain yours?
what use this youth,
this passion and beauty,
if it is to die untasted? un-understood?
wasted! how oft I prayed,
meditated and waited,
then like the sun in July
you came, unappreciated--
oh, what fools we are
to the have the moon and want a star--
it's winter now,
the long short days
are cold and forbearing,
tearing at my very depths
when i think of the summerrhyme,
the short long days,
and the warmth that came and went.

James Tippey
1955

Epistle

Do not cry, my love,
for those who would scoff at life--
whatever the circumstance;

Or those who would mock God--
no matter the consequence;

Or even those who would scorn love,
whether by reason or obstinacy;

For there are those who would search
for beauty though there were no life;

And there are those who would seek
reality though there were no God;

And even those who would hold forth
charity though there were no love . . .
Of these, my love, am I.

Shhhhhh!

Flow not oh gentle tear.
Life hath not yet left you,
and God and love are near.

James Tippey
1955
For Violet

Ode To The Setting Sun

As twilight hovers on the verge of night, a crimson shroud engulfs me where I stand, where I have been, where I envision to go. Alone, I gaze into the face of God.

This is no ordinary sunset, but one that somehow casts a spell, an ominous, eerie aura of finality... as if the warmth of yesterday were left to solace the endless night of eternity.

How is it that so radiant a sphere to sight, and so seemingly omnipresent, can suddenly descend into the abyss of nothingness?

Yet, so searing its imprint on my being, that I am scarred long after the fervor has ceased.

I have seen it, followed it, and reached the length of imagination to embrace it; still, as I succeed, in proportion to my success, I am burned!

For as I am blinded to both line and shape, like primeval forms of life,
have felt its light...and having felt it, may not sustain its loss.

James Tippey
1968

The Children's Home

He drove us to the train depot.
I didn't want to stay.
He led me to my first commode,
and told me I should go,
then flushed my life away.

Each year they took us into town
to get us all some shoes.
They must have bought us other clothes
and things that we could use;
but what they were, who knows?

At Christmas time we sat around
and opened up a gift.
It was the fruit and nigger toes
that I remember most,
for toys did not abound.

Then there was the thunderstorm
that struck one night quite late.
I refused to eat my rice,
and left it on my plate.

The mistress of the girls did warn
that I should stay till it was eaten.
The kinder mistress of the boys
came down to take me up to bed,
although I still had not repented.

But I was young and stubborn,
and sat in that dark room.
I knew that I would not be beaten.
It was a test of will.
Then lightning struck with its loud BOOM!

I didn't eat the rice, I swanned,
but I began to scream;
and the mistress of the boys prevailed.
I would not stay till dawn.
She rescued me; I was redeemed.

There was my friend, his name J.C.
At least that's what I called him.
Then one day it came to me;
his name was really Jesse,
but in my Southern way, I drawled him.

I used to sit out on the grass
and gaze up in the sky.
The clouds all looked like grazing sheep,
migrating when they passed.
I counted them as they went by.

Garland Andrews
1992

Otis

*I moved into a place not long ago
that looks out on the stars.
In going about my daily chores
I seldom venture far.*

*One day I saw a black man
while walking down the hall.
His build is rather stocky,
and he isn't very tall.*

*He catches your eye as you mosey by,
but never invades your space.
The crook of his smile is not out of style
on his kind and gentle face.*

*With hair of salt and pepper,
and appearance quite dapper,
he stands for what is good.*

*They say is name is Otis,
a man you'd hardly notice,
but notice him you should.*

*He's kinda nifty for one nearing fifty,
that comforting way of his.
He puffs on a stogie, not like an old fogy,
but like the gentleman he is.*

*Each month he goes from floor to floor,
the bugman at his side.
Then stands and waits outside the door,
and does it all with pride.*

I've talked with him maybe twice,
in words of wit and spice,
but never probed his mind;

Perhaps it's better not to try,
I wouldn't want to pry -
who knows what I would find?

I never knew an Uncle Tom,
although the state I'm from
must harbor quite a few;

Do-gooders and politically correct
most likely wouldn't connect
with his placid point of view.

If I were black, I'd lack the knack
of putting others at ease.
For I'd be pissed, and shake my fist,
and never want to please.

But that is not the way of Otis,
the man you'd hardly notice,
unless you took the time;

Beneath that calm exterior
is a noble interior
that hints at being sublime.

September 7, 1996

The Father Of Her Child

She was tall and statuesque,
 of stable Anglo stock,
With dark brown hair
 and eyes of mocha chocolate –
  or so I recall.

So she came into my life
 and offered me a choice.
She would care for me and share with me
 the vision (s) of my youth,
  forgetting she was wed.

I never knew just what she saw
 or why she offered me her love;
Perhaps she saw that she wanted to be,
 or wanted me to be
  the father of her child.

In time a girl was born
 with curly hair and sparkling eyes,
  the mirror image of her mother;
With such success, how could I guess
 she'd ever want another?

We tried again a time or two
 as those in love are wont to do,
  but other things were on my mind;
So off I went to hell half-bent
 leaving child and her behind.

It was to be another world,
 a totally different place,

for it was there I found my will;
And though there would be other loves,
  the one I left would haunt me still.

She was a poetess of sorts,
  on Sundays she sang in a choir;
By all reports she was quite good,
  but she would ever strive
    to something even higher.

Her poems were of love and nature,
  of earth, sky and trees;
It was as if the words she wrote
  came from her heart
    and not just meant to please.

But when I left, the essence
  of her world had died –
    she never wrote another word;
At length her voice grew stronger,
  in song if not in verse, I heard.

Her life was proper and mundane,
  she simply tried to cope;
With smile in place upon her face,
  she struggled through a year or two,
    then succumbed to liquid hope.

I thought of her who long ago
  her ways with me beguiled;
She gave to me the gift of praise:
  when at last I held that girl
    I was the father of her child.

        1996 – For Adrienne

*The Long Night Wake**

I waited for the sunset
and for the rain to fall.
I waited for a brand-new day
that never came at all.

Old ways soon grew tiresome;
new ways were never tried.
Nightmares and dreamscapes
were daydreams that died.

The still, small voice of dawning;
God's harbinger of peace,
first echoed in my consciousness,
then gave my soul release.

That long night wake is over;
I find I'm wiser now.
The sunrise and sunset
both look the same somehow.

But the bitterness of loss,
the exhilaration of gain;
have made my psyche better,
and so it shall remain.

1997

The Countess of Manhattan

There was a bygone time
when people showed respect.
When everyone knew their place,
not just the place of others.

While doting fathers and mothers
designed to be denied,
it was their child's accomplishments
that were their source of pride.

It was a simple time
when titles still had meaning.
Everyone was Sir or Ma'am, and
youngsters seldom sassed a grownup.

If they were bad, few dared to own up;
for no one cared to spare the rod.
With no incentive to complain, they
braced themselves and bore the pain.

This was when she lived; a woman of her
age with dignity in her face and
garments that were tattered.

She knew what really mattered
was how she held her head,
the way she moved about
each night when she went out.

No one asked her name.
They simply called her Countess;
a title used in jest.

And then there was her faithful guide
who never left her side.
Was he husband, count, or knave?
There was no cause to know;
she kept him well in tow.

They came into the diner,
the countess and her mate.
They had no reservation,
but took an empty table.

She looked to see what was available,
then reached for one thin dime
and ordered coffee for two;
for them one cup would do.

She need not see the menu;
the fare was in full view,
sitting there for her to take,
smooshed together on a bus.

Then she scraped with little fuss
the courses of their feast:
mashed potatoes, burger or fish,
biscuits and gravy, beans or quiche.

Back to the table she would go
to set before her beau.
The coffee she bought was not too hot.
He'd drink it soon enough.

With greasy spoons they ate the stuff,
their humble night's repast...

*If tomorrow's pickings weren't so good,
that meal would have to last.*

*As they partook of the table scraps,
no other thought ensued.
While most engaged in idle chat,
the countess and her friend,
in such dire need none need pretend –
they were there to eat.*

*For all the splendor they did lack,
you knew they'd soon be back.
Few could know just where she lived
or where she hung her hat;
whether hovel or uptown flat.*

*But as they went into the night,
their journey wasn't far from sight.
For it was bitter cold,
their clothes were none to warm,
and they were very old.*

*By now she must be dead,
so many years ago.
She played her role upon that stage;
did someone take her place?*

*As for name or state of grace,
whatever is written in stone,
it was the Countess of Manhattan
by which that lady was known.*

1997

Impersonal Acquaintance

*I saw a man the other day
who seemed to be going
a different way.*

*But when I asked
he wouldn't stay.
So I never learned
what he had to say.*

*Then I saw myself
as he walked away.*

December 21, 1997

Mother-Child

Good morning, mother.
How alive you look today.

You seem so staid and demure with your
youthful face enframed in leather... now
an eight-by-ten reconstruction in sepia;
it brings the look together.

When last I found you mother, you were
on a snapshot much smaller than a
postcard. With dress torn and hair wind-
blown, who would have know you
standing with your brother?

But then we uplifted you, raised you to a
loftier height, and cleansed you head to
toe. We sewed your dress, combed your
hair, and left you standing there
in the middle of the studio.

Smile, sweet mother.
This is how I remember you.

They say you were eleven, and that was
only seven years before you went to
heaven, or wherever loving mothers go.

But when I see you, you have the
countenance of a woman; a Mona Lisa
sadness in your smile.

*I like to think that smile was meant for
me, though I know it can't be so –
I would not come yet for a while.*

*Some years ago I wrote an organ piece;
I called it "Consummation";
whereas it was a bit presumptuous,
to me it expressed the summation,
the epitome of all you were.*

*For you were the consummate and
ever-caring mother;
the guarding angel of my life.*

*You hardly had time to be a child, and yet
with all your strife you were a precious
mother-child.*

*I have a fleeting recollection of walking to
a church. There was someone else beside us
and she was young like you.*

*Straddling furrows deep and wide,
entrenched in dry eroded ground,
you took your firm and gentle hand
and guided me across each mound.*

*Then while we were inside, twilight was
encroaching. Was it a prescient vision of
your approaching night?*

*Pray, blessed mother.
God will hear your prayers.*

And then there was the final trip.
You bundled me, my brother,
and with an aunt just twelve years old,
father drove to take us there...
in a car run-down and ill-equipped
for winter's frigid air.

The weather was dank and dreary,
there was no heater, nor shattered
windshield since removed.

This was all best left unspoken, for what
you most behooved was seeing your folks
again.

Welcome home sweet angel.
It's nice to see you now and then.

It was to be your present.
You were a Yuletide child and
longed to visit your past.

But then within one day,
your ten-and-eight birthday,
fever rose and you breathed your last.

Happy birthday, mother.
There will never be another.

You were so very young, so frail and thin,
and that's how I remember you.
I see you in my hands, my chin, my eyes,
and even in the hair of my head.

But most of all it was the presence of you
while you were here, and I was there close
to the warmth of you, on your last bed.

And then I closed my eyes –
there was no need to fear.
The next thing I remember,
you were lying on your bier.

They say it was pneumonia or possibly
consumption, but is it so important?
It's all based on assumption that with
proper care something could be done.
But what use are postmortems when you
are three, and your mother-child is gone?

Even now, after all these years,
it elicits dormant tears,
for the trauma lingers on.

That was my first real mourning, but we
would stay together and we would pray.
We had the ties that bind, the primordial
glue – we would await a better day.

But even ties can be broken, families torn
asunder for lack of token will.
Is it any wonder? For though it was rare,
still times were harder then.

How oft I felt remorse and guilt –
why should I live when you could not?
Now all that remains of the world
you knew is a bleak, deserted plot.

There is no simple tombstone,
no plaque or wooden marker.
I only know who lies within
by your position in a line
beside your mother and father...
Could the next one be mine?

But before I live my final days –
they assess my worth and sing my praise –
I pray the last thing I shall see
will be your youthful face and smile
meant just for me.

Goodnight, dear mother.
For soon I sleep with you.

1997
For Mary Smith Busby
(December 24, 1916 – December 24, 1934)

Born 100 years before Garland passed.

The Very Touch of You

As I look at your picture today,
   I think of the things we did
      and the places we went not long ago.

Of the time you touched my hand in awe,
   and the way you caressed my hair.
I lived for those times together
   and the love we briefly shared –
      more than you could ever know.

Of all the loves I've known –
   from adolescence to you –
      yours is the one that will endure.
You had a transcendent beauty
     and inner glow that radiated beyond
       an aura, and reflected in my smile.
I hope that glow will never change and be
   the same both yesterday and tomorrow.

The tenderness of your touch,
   the electricity of your eyes
      could warm my heart, enflame
       desire, and set my soul on fire.

Time again I've asked myself,
   "Why did it end?" No single
      answer came up twice.
The hardest thing I ever did
   was to say good-bye to you.

I tried to pretend that I was stoic,
   that your love no longer phased me.

But it was no use, somehow you knew –
   I couldn't even be heroic.

There are times when to save ourselves
   we must extricate and purge our souls;
Because the hurt is so intense
   that emotions flood and leave us numb
     to our very core –
      that was such a time.

The tears I wept and the words I wrote
   bespeak of that disappointment –
They sound disillusioned and bitter.

I can reason that you have grown in size
   and are beginning to show your years.
But that doesn't erase the pain
   and it doesn't dry the tears –
There is no cure for that.

One night I said, while in your arms,
   that I wanted to die that way –
I doubt that you believed me.

And while I may not go that way,
   I will never forget your touch.
I hope that somehow you'll remember
   I love you so very much –
More than you'll ever know.

              August 23, 1997
              For Ginny

San Francisco Rose

I met her on a cable car
while staying in San Francisco
and playing at the Geary.
Her name was Rose; she made an
impression when she struck a pose,
and her disposition was cheery.

She wasn't a princess or a beauty queen,
or anything in-between, by far;
But with her sexy routine in
in a costume so sheen,
she might have been a star.
Nor was she as gorgeous, I think,
as her younger sister, Molly.

Her face shone plainly,
she was lithesome and gainly,
but her body would stop a truck.
She swayed and pranced whenever she
danced, and her breasts stayed up by luck.

She and her baby sister appeared at the
club next door, where both were go-go
dancers, or what was know as topless;
though why they called it that,
I wouldn't presume to guess.

What flared above her waist,
without silicone or paste,
was so amply endowed that when she

*gave out, there still was plenty more.
After the show one night,
an eager fiend and I decided to stop over
and have a drink or two,
when there in full sight was the girl
named Rose I met not long before.*

*We watched for a while till she gave us a
smile, then came and sat beside us...
And there she did abide us.
As if anticipating, she asked us to her pad;
Her sibling would be waiting.
With news like that, who could be sad?*

*For there I first smoked grass, and exposed
myself to the psychedelic fad.
Without ado or fuss,
she changed into something less,
though far more comfortable – for her, if
not for us – then put on a private dance.*

*Young Molly, alone on a cushioned floor
mat, in semi-trance, read from a poetry
book.*

*Rose offered us wine, Red Mountain rosé,
played guitar and sitar L.P.'s,
and asked if we would stay.*

*Between hashish and dew, it was all we
could do to keep our hands at bay.
Without second thought, a girl we each
caught – he in one room, I another.*

The women, it seemed, had already
schemed and treated us more like lovers,
than new-made friends or brothers.

We greeted the morning a lot less horny,
but soon I left for L.A.
She was killed not long after in a traffic
disaster, her image since faded and died.

I'll never forget the Geary, the go-go club
not far from the stage door side,
her cheery demeanor, the day we met
on a clanging cable car, nor the night I
stayed and went, half-high and fully spent,
with her sister, Molly.

And to this day, since I moved away,
I think of her always as
San Francisco's dancing and prancing
Rose of Trolley.

1998

The Lucid Pool

*I stand beside a lucid pool not far from my
best friend; alone because I choose to be,
because I cannot be with him,
except to kneel before his grave.*

*So many thoughts stir within,
some of which we used to share;
But there is something deeper here:
the pool of life from which we sprang.*

*Now in the sunset of my life,
and the eternal night of his,
ephemeral kinship is evoked.*

*I shall well remember this time,
long after we are gone--
he to his place, I to mine;
Only the pool will then remain.*

1998

The Image of Me

*I glance in the mirror
and what do I see?
The face of a man
resembling me.
I turn on the radio
and what do I hear?
My voice recorded
in a bygone year.
I rise to the ceiling
and look on a bed.
There lies a hull
deserted and bled –
The face, the voice
the body are one;
As planets and moons
are part of the sun.
Each has its purpose,
its given routine;
Till death intervenes
and lays them supine.
The face is now ashen,
the voice has gone mute;
The body is lifeless,
the brain not astute.
The soul goes aloft,
the corpse stays behind.
All that remains –
a ghost to remind.*

September 14, 1999

Eros' Wine

A tad, I knew the love of mother-child.
Then with her death, it was defiled
as I sought love in female form –
with bouncing hair and sparkling eyes,
in skirts that rose up to their thighs.
But empty love leaves empty hearts
(an unsung message quite apart).
And while their kind are soft and warm,
they're doldrums ports in bruising storms.

As I matured and took account,
those loves had left me flat, I found;
For I had drunk of love's new wine,
and drained it all from Eros' vat.
The sampled vessels tasted fine;
But as I emptied each full glass,
its famed elixir did not last.
A prescient wake-up call in time,
it really didn't matter that. . .

There is no magic potion or secret means
of finding love. For while it seems
elusive and somewhat out of grasp,
once we search within our hearts,
and gain the courage to like ourselves,
that's when we open up to others
and leave room for new love to start.
And though it is an arduous task,
it is this act that makes us lovers.

September 23, 1999

The Road Less Traveled

Take the road well traveled
for fewer challenges and simpler goals,
security and minimum misadventure,
and walk in comfort till you die;

Or scale the rugged mountains high,
struggle toward life's real adventure,
plumb earth's depths with kindred souls—
That's the road less traveled.

August 27, 2000

*Peccavi**

I have sinned...
  By doing what was wrong by you
  and not doing what was right;
I have lied...
  By overstating my attributes
  and undervaluing yours;
I have robbed...
  You of your youth
  and offered back old age;
I have cheated...
  By failing to show you
  the respect you deserved;
I have killed...
  The love you had for me
  by wasting it on another;
I have been selfish...
  By taking all you had
  and giving little in return;
I have been unfaithful...
  By sharing with others
  what I withheld from you;
Yes, I have done these things – and more...
  But by your forgiveness
  a love has been redeemed.

  August 27, 2000
  For Ginny

Silent Pleas

*Do not doubt my love, my dear,
for love with doubt will not fulfill.
Where doubt resides, love can't abide,
and doubt remains there still.*

*Look into my tear-filled eyes,
stripped of all their vain pretense.
My life is there for you to read,
and leaves me no defense.*

*Listen to my silent please,
the muffled whispers of despair.
Musings of a trampled heart
were once imprisoned there.*

*The open wound I languished from
has healed, the scar long disappeared.
Your warm embrace has eased concern
for everything I feared.*

*So take the hand I lay in yours;
the phalanx of my mortal quest.
Then raise it to your tender lips
and clasp it to your breast.*

*Do not doubt my love, my dear,
for doubt and love shall never meet.
When doubt departs, love fills the heart;
the cycle is complete.*

*August 27, 2000
For Ginny*

To Valeria

You are like a spark of light
set off in a dark room:
I see things I no longer
knew were there,
I feel emotions that had
long been dormant.

I see where I am going,
I understand where I have been.
There is no past or future,
only the immediacy of the present.

I am neither young nor old,
but free of time's constraints;
eager to begin anew where reason
dictated I should leave off -
(what was once lost is foreordained
not to be lost again).

Turn not your face from me,
for your light illumines my soul.
In this labyrinth of life
there is only one way out.

Take not your light from me
that I must wander alone.
Leave me content to meet
life's ultimate destiny.

Amen.
March 15, 2011

Two Girls Went To Church

Two girls went to church one day;
a virgin and a whore.
They each believed that if she changed
she'd be accepted more.

They both had sought a different style;
a welcome change of pace.
The one went on to mend her ways;
the other fell from grace.

The virgin asked that she might
for once be action free;
uninhibited like the rest,
and choose her company.

When she got what she had sought;
at first she was content.
But once she fit within the crowd,
no virgin could repent.

The other girl, as she would learn,
could not outlive the past.
It was her sordid reputation;
the one thing that would last.

The truth she lost or never learned,
if once she ever knew;
whatever thing that she might want,
she would in time eschew.

*This is the advice the priest intoned,
though not unto to her face:
"Be careful of the things you ask –
Hail Mary, full of grace."*

August, 2013

A Walk in the Sun

Love is like the pristine sky
Bestowed on everyone;
And while at times the clouds roll by,
They only hide the sun--
Each day enhances what's begun.

The warmth exists for us to take
And nourish the frail soul;
Its harmful rays lie in their wake
Unless we take control--
While nothing takes its toll.

I used to walk out in the shade,
Or often stay inside;
I never knew that blossoms fade
And flowers sometimes died
without the love those days provide...

Until you came into my life
And made me feel alive;
You took away all needless strife
And forced me to survive--
The very thing for which we strive.

Now I walk out in the sun
With you there by my side;
The menial tasks of life are fun,
These I do with pride--
All other manners have been tried.

So take my hand and lead me on
The walk down Sunny Lane;
I'll stay with you till life is done
And memories remain . . .
Or fate unites us once again.

August 15, 2013
For Valerie

Dogs and Cats

Dogs are man's best friend,
   sages long have said;
They come in all dimensions now
   depending how their bred.

They're found in every country,
   island, or atoll;
When times are bad, although it's sad,
   they're in a dinner bowl.

They like to go for walks each day
   along a favorite trail;
They greet their friends along the way
   and check the day's p-mail.

Dogs have but a single life
   while cats seem to have nine;
But dogs can do more in one life
   than nine of a feline.

They've even written songs for dogs--
   never for a cat;
When taken altogether it shows
   where their worth is at.

But then there are those special needs,
   requiring much attention;
They need fences, ropes and leashes
   to keep them in detention.

You must adhere to their time schedule--
  never to your own--
You can't go out for very long
  and leave the mutt alone.

They seem to bark incessantly
  at everything in sight;
They yip and growl for your protection
  and do it day and night.

Their behavior can be crude
  when others come to call;
They lick one end and sniff the other --
  such manners do appall.

For what attention they may show,
  it comes at a dear price--
They eat you out of house and home . . .
  and heart to be precise.

So when all things are considered,
  it's really tit for tat;
Some people simply like a dog,
  while others like a cat.

August 14, 2013

Parrots
or Tribute to Mozart

If you use a naughty word
in earshot of a parrot;
don't be surprised if someday soon
he'll more than likely share it.

It seems they live for fifty years,
often past their folks;
their antics tend to make you laugh
and are the brunt of jokes.

Mozey pecks on old wine corks
and grapes still in the raw;
but when he perches on your hand,
he sometimes pecks your paw.

He'll screech and squawk for what he
wants -- midday treats or toys;
you may be sure whate'er it is,
he'll get it soon with noise.

Though you may want a quiet pet
as docile as a kitten;
yet when it makes a funny quip,
that bird will leave you smitten.

October 23, 2013
For Valerie

Thoughts Worth Repeating

Some thoughts are worth repeating and become more relevant as time progresses. I wish to repeat one now: "I love you for what you have done, and not for what you have not done." You have had many and varied experiences, and I long to give you more. I find it exciting that you are receptive to new adventures and even daring experiments. As our relationship grows and matures, my feelings for you increase and give me a flood of new ideas and perspectives. You are the most complete individual I have ever known; yet forever willing to expand. Your unparalleled beauty and talent are but the shell of the core of your true being. You are a work of art, and should be appreciated and enjoyed by all. When I die I want to bask in the realization that I was a part of you and you were a part of me. What I have given you, you have equally given me. With that in mind, I will rest in peace. I love you Valerie, as I have loved no other. -Garland

November 11, 203
For Valerie

Dearest Love,

*I love you for who you are, and not for whom you might pretend to be;
I love you for your freedom and previous exploits, and not for your hidden inhibitions;
I love you for your delicate balance between moral turpitude and feigned innocence;
I love you for seeking new experiences, and not just for taking comfort in old ones;
I love you for your openness,
your willingness to share
your deepest emotions,
and not for withholding the ugliness and trauma from your past;
I love you for your trust, your lack of skepticism concerning my intentions and love for you.
I love you for your faith in me,
your appraisal of what I have been,
and your patience with what I might become. -Garland*

> *November 8, 2013*
> *Far Valerie*

Return And Farewell

I stand nearby and wave
as she drives away —
taking my heart along.

Where then did she come
from ages long ago
to touch me as she may?

Her woeful life in sum
is hidden deep in song —
of this we are but one.

What has she ever done
in all those bygone years
that made her what she is?

What were her vanished hopes,
her triumphs and defeats,
her faded joys and tears?

These things I cannot know,
though she bared them all
and shared them openly.

Yet what she freely gave
has made her dearer still —
a tale most rife with pain.

And these I hold within
until she comes again —
for love her I always will.

December 12, 2013 - For Valerie

End of the Line

*There were those ahead of me
   and others in a line;
There were also more behind me,
   but that to me was fine.*

*Still at times, events remind me
   of those days gone by;
You were a young and pretty thing --
   I dared not even try.*

*Of all the lovelies then and now,
   you were the fairest being;
Yet countless ones who vied somehow
   you ended up not seeing.*

*Most suitors were tall, a few less so --
   I was in-between;
Some for pride, some for show,
   the handsomest to be seen.*

*As for the amount, whatever the count,
   whether by fate or by design,
When all are taken into account,
   I was the end of the line.*

         December 28, 2013
         For Valerie

Gifts of the Magi

Sing to me a worthy song —
not of unrequited love, nor of common
platitudes, but one of untold verities
and newfound attitudes.

Bring to me your precious gifts —
not worldly trinkets, but those of Magi,
befitting neither child nor man,
symbolic of the cross: INRI,
part of God's eternal plan.

Stay with me yet for a while --
not until a new day breaks,
but till I draw my final breath,
and with that breath bestow a blessing
before I lie prostrate in death.

This is what I want from you --
not cliché words and saccharin tunes,
but all the things I truly lack:
gifts you freely give to me,
and in my passing give them back.

January 27, 2014
For Valerie

Many Wondrous Sounds

Dry kisses wafted on the sly
Brown eyes probing limpid blue
Fingers touch like Adam and God
Golden hair in loose cascade
Upraised hands wave sad adieu
As tears well up and overflow

Snow falling in the night
Waking to a special day
The first ray of pending dawn
The pause before the thunderclap
The primal surge of a novel thought
And the heart aflutter with new love

March 16, 2014
For Valerie

A Zephyr In The Spring

Like a zephyr in the spring
she came into his life.
An echo from an era past
when they were full of zeal;
ere each had been through mortal strife
and witnessed pangs of death.

But there had been a common bond
unspoken from the start.
And though long years had intervened,
an image lingered in her heart.
For they were two souls much in tune
and chordal in their part.

What was a meet unto the one
was well-met by the other.
Emotions grew with each encounter
and trust in one another.
The depth that shone within her eyes
was for that special one.

Now if their story can be told,
she was young and he was old.
What they had was brief in years,
yet like a river through a pass,
their love was deeper than both sides.
And with a lunar tide of tears --
the memory of that love abides.

April 30, 2014
For Valerie

My Darling Valerie,

You are everything I want in a woman.
You are beautiful, and though you are
aware of your beauty,
you are not consumed by it;

You are young and vivacious,
and if I cannot keep up with you,
it is not because of your over-expectations,
but my shortcomings;

You are intelligent and talented,
though you have not realized your
potential;

You are tender and kind,
yet firm in your resolve;

You are experienced, yet un-jaded
and naive as to its significance;

You are giving, yet undemanding of
receiving;

You are FREE from societal mores,
yet constrained by an inner morality;

You are spiritual, yet not fanatically
religious;

You are eternally optimistic
against all odds and naysayers.

Taken altogether, you are the most wonderful person in my life.

I shall always love you for it!

Gratefully yours,

Garland
February 1, 2015

Reasons I Love You

I love you for who you are,
  not for who you might have been.
I love you for your lack of fear,
  not for pretense courage.
I love you for your fragile balance
  between moral turpitude
    and feigned innocence . . .
I love you for seeking new trials,
  not for taking comfort in the old.
I love you for your openness and
  ability to share the pain of trauma
    from the past.
I love you for your trust, your lack of
  doubt concerning my intentions
    and love for you.
I love you for your faith in me,
  your approval of what I have done,
    and patience with what I might
      become.

          September 16, 2016
            For Valerie

Love of mine,

*I have little to say except that you are
special, you are precious.
You are tender, loving and kind;
you are generous to a fault.
You are beautiful,
but you do not flaunt your beauty.
You have suffered much, which makes you
sensitive to the pain of others.
You strive for perfection where
others accept mediocrity.
You are both intuitive and analytical.
You have accomplished much, but are
humble in your achievements.
You are an eternal optimist;
for you no obstacle is insurmountable.
You are spiritual, but you do not sacrifice
the blessings of this world.
You are faithful to an ideal,
though others may condemn you.
You love with your heart and soul,
expecting little in return.
Your talents know no limitation.
And finally, you are a complete being
capable of giving of yourself
and still remaining whole.
I thank the gods for allowing you
to come to me at this point in my life.
I love you, Valerie. -Garland*

November 26, 2016

www.ingramcontent.com/pod-product-compliance
Lightning Source LLC
Chambersburg PA
CBHW031409040426
42444CB00005B/488